S0-AJS-331
SEP 23 20

STOP!

You may be reading the wrong way!

NO LONGER PROPERTY OF
SEATTLE PUBLIC LIBRARY

In keeping with the original Japanese comic format, this book reads from right to left—so word balloons, action, and sound effects and are reversed to preserve the orientation of the original artwork.

Check out the diagram shown here to get the hang of things, and then turn to the other side of the book to get started!

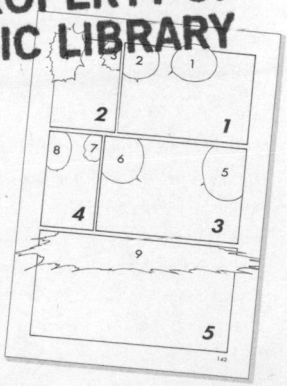

THE INSPIRATION FOR THE ANIME

Yona of the Dawn

Story & Art by
Mizuho Kusanagi

Princess Yona lives an ideal life as the only princess of her kingdom. Doted on by her father, the king, and protected by her faithful guard Hak, she cherishes the time spent with the man she loves, Su-won. But everything changes on her 16th birthday when tragedy strikes her family!

Shojo Beat
shojobeat.com

viz media
viz.com

RATED T FOR TEEN

Akatsuki no Yona © Mizuho Kusanagi 2010/ HAKUSENSHA, Inc.

TO SAVE HER KINGDOM, A SIMPLE VILLAGE GIRL MUST LIVE A ROYAL LIE.

PRINCE Freya

Story and Art by
KEIKO ISHIHARA

The powerful kingdom of Sigurd has slowly been conquering all the lands that share its borders, and now it has turned its voracious attention to the small, resource-rich Tyr. Tyr cannot hope to match Sigurd in strength, so in order to survive, it must rely on the intelligence, skill and cunning of its prince and his loyal knights. But should their prince fall, so too shall Tyr...

Itsuwari no Freya © Keiko Ishihara 2018/HAKUSENSHA, Inc.

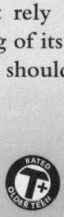

VIZ

FROM THE CREATOR OF
VAMPIRE KNIGHT

Shuriken and Pleats

When the master she has sworn to protect is killed, Mikage Kirio, a skilled ninja, travels to Japan to start a new, peaceful life for herself. But as soon as she arrives, she finds herself fighting to protect the life of Mahito Wakashimatsu, a man who is under attack by a band of ninja. From that time on, Mikage is drawn deeper into the machinations of his powerful family.

Shojo Beat viz media www.viz.com

RATED T TEEN ratings.viz.com

Shuriken to Pleats © Matsuri Hino 2015/HAKUSENSHA, Inc.

Uncover the secrets of the **NIGHT CLASS**

$14.99 US $19.99 CAN* | 978-1-4215-3238-7

VAMPIRE KNIGHT

OFFICIAL FANBOOK

By Matsuri Hino

Get juicy details on the **hottest vampire** student body with the **OFFICIAL FANBOOK**. Complete with:

- Character design sketches and storyboards
- Cross Academy student ID card
- Glossy color pages
- Exclusive interview with the creator

Available at your local bookstore or comic store.

Shojo Beat
www.shojobeat.com

Vampire Knight © Matsuri Hino 2004/HAKUSENSHA, Inc.
Vampire Knight Koushiki Fanbook X © Matsuri Hino 2008/HAKUSENSHA, Inc.
* Prices subject to change

VAMPIRE KNIGHT: MEMORIES
Vol. 7
Shojo Beat Edition

STORY AND ART BY
MATSURI HINO

Adaptation/Nancy Thistlethwaite
Translation/Tetsuichiro Miyaki
Touch-Up Art & Lettering/Inori Fukuda Trant
Graphic Design/Alice Lewis
Editor/Nancy Thistlethwaite

Vampire Knight memories by Matsuri Hino © Matsuri Hino 2021
All rights reserved. First published in Japan in 2021 by HAKUSENSHA, Inc., Tokyo. English language translation rights arranged with HAKUSENSHA, Inc., Tokyo.

The stories, characters, and incidents mentioned in this publication are entirely fictional.

No portion of this book may be reproduced or transmitted in any form or by any means without written permission from the copyright holders.

Printed in the U.S.A.

Published by VIZ Media, LLC
P.O. Box 77010
San Francisco, CA 94107

10 9 8 7 6 5 4 3 2 1
First printing, July 2022

PARENTAL ADVISORY
VAMPIRE KNIGHT: MEMORIES is rated T+ for Older Teen and is recommended for ages 16 and up. This volume contains sexual themes.

viz.com

shojobeat.com

Matsuri Hino burst onto the manga scene with her title *Kono Yume ga Sametara* (When This Dream Is Over), which was published in *LaLa DX* magazine. Hino was a manga artist a mere nine months after she decided to become one.

With the success of her popular series *Captive Hearts*, *MeruPuri*, and *Vampire Knight*, Hino is a major player in the world of shojo manga.

Hino enjoys creative activities and has commented that she would have been either an architect or an apprentice to traditional Japanese craftsmasters if she had not become a manga artist.

恋

Ren

Ren means "love." It is used in terms of a romantic love or crush.

藍堂星夜

Aido Seiya

Aido means "indigo temple." *Sei* means "star" and *ya* means "night": "starry night."

Terms

-sama: The suffix *-sama* is used in formal address for someone who ranks higher in the social hierarchy. The vampires call their leader "Kaname-sama" only when they are among their own kind.

縹木

Hanadagi

In this family name, *hanada* means "bright light blue" and *gi* means "tree."

影山霞

Kageyama Kasumi

In the Class Rep's family name, *kage* means "shadow" and *yama* means "mountain." His first name, *Kasumi*, means "haze" or "mist."

愛

Ai

Ai means "love." It is used in terms of unconditional, unending love and affection.

菖藤依砂也

Shoto Isaya

Sho means "Siberian iris" and *to* is "wisteria." The *I* in *Isaya* means "to rely on" while the *sa* means "sand." *Ya* is a suffix used for emphasis.

橙茉

Toma

In the family name *Toma*, *to* means "Seville orange" and *ma* means "jasmine flower."

藍堂永路

Aido Nagamichi

The name *Nagamichi* is a combination of *naga*, which means "long" or "eternal," and *michi*, which is the kanji for "road" or "path." *Aido* means "indigo temple."

玖蘭樹里

Kuran Juri

Kuran means "nine orchids." In her first name, *ju* means "tree" and a *ri* is a traditional Japanese unit of measure for distance. The kanji for *ri* is the same as in Senri's name.

玖蘭悠

Kuran Haruka

Kuran means "nine orchids." *Haruka* means "distant" or "remote."

鷹宮海斗

Takamiya Kaito

Taka means "hawk" and *miya* means "imperial palace" or "shrine." *Kai* is "sea" and *to* means "to measure" or "grid."

白蕗更

Shirabuki Sara

Shira is "white" and *buki* is "butterbur," a plant with white flowers. *Sara* means "to renew."

黒主灰閻

Cross Kaien

Cross, or *Kurosu*, means "black master." *Kaien* is a combination of *kai*, meaning "ashes," and *en*, meaning "village gate." The kanji for *en* is also used for Enma, the ruler of the underworld in Buddhist mythology.

玖蘭李土

Kuran Rido

Kuran means "nine orchids." In *Rido*, *ri* means "plum" and *do* means "earth."

錐生壱縷

Kiryu Ichiru

Ichi is the old-fashioned way of writing "one," and *ru* means "thread." In *Kiryu*, the *ki* means "auger" or "drill" and the *ryu* means "life."

緋桜閑, 狂咲姫

Hio Shizuka, Kuruizaki-hime

Shizuka means "calm and quiet." In Shizuka's family name, *hi* is "scarlet" and *ou* is "cherry blossoms." Shizuka Hio is also referred to as the "Kuruizaki-hime." *Kuruizaki* means "flowers blooming out of season" and *hime* means "princess."

藍堂月子

Aido Tsukiko

Aido means "indigo temple." *Tsukiko* means "moon child."

星煉

Seiren

Sei means "star" and *ren* means "to smelt" or "to refine." *Ren* is also the same kanji used in *rengoku*, or "purgatory." Her previous name, *Hoshino*, uses the same kanji for "star" (*hoshi*) and *no*, which can mean "from" and is often used at the end of traditional female names.

遠矢莉磨

Toya Rima

Toya means a "far-reaching arrow." Rima's first name is a combination of *ri*, or "jasmine," and *ma*, which signifies enhancement by wearing away, such as by polishing or scouring.

紅まり亜

Kurenai Maria

Kurenai means "crimson." The kanji for the last *a* in Maria's first name is the same that is used in "Asia."

夜刈十牙

Yagari Toga

Yagari is a combination of *ya*, meaning "night," and *gari*, meaning "to harvest." *Toga* means "ten fangs."

一条麻遠,一翁

Ichijo Asato, a.k.a. "Ichio"

Ichijo can mean a "ray" or "streak." Asato's first name is comprised of *asa*, meaning "hemp" or "flax," and *tou*, meaning "far-off." His nickname is *ichi*, or "one," combined with *ou*, which can be used as an honorific when referring to an older man.

若葉沙頼

Wakaba Sayori

Yori's full name is Sayori Wakaba. *Wakaba* means "young leaves." Her given name, *Sayori*, is a combination of *sa*, meaning "sand," and *yori*, meaning "trust."

早園瑠佳

Souen Ruka

In *Ruka*, the *ru* means "lapis lazuli" while the *ka* means "good-looking" or "beautiful." The *sou* in Ruka's surname, *Souen*, means "early," but this kanji also has an obscure meaning of "strong fragrance." The *en* means "garden."

一条拓麻

Ichijo Takuma

Ichijo can mean a "ray" or "streak." The kanji for *Takuma* is a combination of *taku*, meaning "to cultivate," and *ma*, which is the kanji for *asa*, meaning "hemp" or "flax," a plant with blue flowers.

支葵千里

Shiki Senri

Shiki's last name is a combination of *shi*, meaning "to support," and *ki*, meaning "mallow"—a flowering plant with pink or white blossoms. The *ri* in *Senri* is a traditional Japanese unit of measure for distance, and one *ri* is about 2.44 miles. *Senri* means "1,000 *ri*."

玖蘭枢

Kuran Kaname

Kaname means "hinge" or "door." The kanji for his last name is a combination of the old-fashioned way of writing *ku*, meaning "nine," and *ran*, meaning "orchid": "nine orchids."

藍堂英

Aido Hanabusa

Hanabusa means "petals of a flower." *Aido* means "indigo temple." In Japanese, the pronunciation of *Aido* is very close to the pronunciation of the English word *idol*.

架院暁

Kain Akatsuki

Akatsuki means "dawn" or "day break." In *Kain, ka* is a base or support, while *in* denotes a building that has high fences around it, such as a temple or school.

EDITOR'S NOTES

CHARACTERS

Matsuri Hino puts careful thought into the names of her characters in *Vampire Knight*. Below is the collection of characters throughout the manga. Each character's name is presented family name first, per the kanji reading.

黒主優姫

Cross Yuki

Yuki's last name, *Kurosu*, is the Japanese pronunciation of the English word "cross." However, the kanji has a different meaning—*kuro* means "black" and *su* means "master." Her first name is a combination of *yuu*, meaning "tender" or "kind," and *ki*, meaning "princess."

錐生零

Kiryu Zero

Zero's first name is the kanji for *rei*, meaning "zero." In his last name, *Kiryu*, the *ki* means "auger" or "drill" and the *ryu* means "life."

Thank you to my assistants and everyone who helped make volume 7 possible: O. Mio-sama, A. Ichiya-sama. And to all you readers, thank you very much from the bottom of my heart!

Hino

REN'S HONEY/END

TIME PASSES SO QUICKLY.

LEAVING ASIDE FOR A MOMENT THE QUESTION OF WHETHER IT'S POSSIBLE OR NOT...
...YOU MAKE IT SOUND AS THOUGH THE QUICKEST WAY TO PEACE IS FOR YOU TO BECOME EMPEROR.
THAT'S RIGHT.
AND I'LL DO IT...
...QUEEN OF THE VAMPIRES.

AFTER BEING SAVED, HE'D FOUND SHELTER WITH THE RESIS-TANCE ARMY.
HE'D ASKED THE LEADER OF THAT ARMY, MARIA KURENAI, IF HE COULD MEET ME.
HE TOOK THAT RISK SO WE COULD DISCUSS IF THERE WERE ANY OTHER WAY BEFORE THE RESISTANCE EXECUTED THEIR PLAN.
THE YOUNG BOY I'D SAVED TEN YEARS AGO...
...WAS THE THIRD PRINCE, THE ONE WHO SUPPOSEDLY HAD BEEN ASSASSI-NATED BY THE EMPEROR.
WHAT A SURPRISE. I DID SENSE THAT BOY WAS HIDING SOMETHING, BUT...

IT'S BEEN TEN YEARS SINCE THEN.
REN STILL HASN'T RETURNED.
SHE SENDS ME A CUTE LETTER EVERY NOW AND THEN.
TO BE HONEST, I MISS HER SO MUCH...
I'VE COME TO ASK YOU IF THERE'S ANY POSSIBILITY OF PEACE BETWEEN US...
...IF I WERE TO BECOME THE FUTURE EMPEROR.
BUT I HAVE A BIGGER PROBLEM TO FOCUS ON.

I'M SO HAPPY THAT I WAS FINALLY ABLE TO SHARE THAT JOY WITH YOU...
REN LEFT AFTER TELLING ME THAT.

ISN'T HOW WE FEEL NOW...
...ENOUGH ...?

I'M A SCARY ADULT BEAST IN HUMAN SKIN TOO.
I DON'T WANT TO STEAL EVEN THE SLIGHTEST AMOUNT...
...OF YOUR LIFE SPAN.
I KNOW YOU CARE FOR ME A GREAT DEAL, AI.
I FEEL THE SAME WAY ABOUT YOU.

SUFF
SUFF
DON'T BE SCARED.

THAT BEAST WANTED TO DEVOUR YOU DOWN TO YOUR BONES.
OUR PARENTS SURELY NOTICED, BUT THEY STILL ENTRUSTED YOU TO ME.
THAT'S WHY I DE-CIDED...
...I MUST ALWAYS PROTECT YOU FROM ME.
Ai.

THE EMOTION I FELT THE FIRST TIME WE CONNECTED...
IT WAS ONLY FOR A MOMENT...
...BUT IT WAS MORE THAN ENOUGH.
YOUR THIN, PALE SKIN...
I COULD SMELL YOUR FRAGRANCE FROM UN-DERNEATH IT...
THE BEAST WITHIN ME WAS TREMBLING WITH JOY.

EVERY TIME YOU DRINK MY BLOOD I CAN SENSE IT.
I KNOW YOU'RE SO THIRSTY FOR MY BLOOD THAT YOU CAN'T BEAR IT.
YOU HOLD BACK BECAUSE YOU'RE SCARED.

EVEN LAST NIGHT...
...I COULD TELL...
...YOU WERE HAVING TROUBLE HOLDING YOURSELF BACK.
YOU...
IT'S ABOUT TIME YOU TASTED ME.

WILL YOU BE ABLE TO BEAR IT...
...FOR SO LONG...?
WHAT A SILLY GIRL.
YOU'RE SAYING ALL THIS BECAUSE YOU WANT ME TO BITE YOU.
THAT'S TRUE.
AFTER ALL, IT'S SPECIAL FOR YOU, RIGHT?
GRIP

I KNOW YOU'RE HUNGRY, AI.
...
YOU'VE ALWAYS...
...BEEN HUNGRY. ALWAYS.
EVER SINCE I WAS BORN.

I WON'T LET YOU GO.
I PROBABLY WON'T BE BACK FOR SOME TIME.
OTHERWISE I WOULDN'T WANT YOU TO DOTE ON ME.
BUT IT WILL PROBABLY BE A VERY, VERY LONG TIME.

KA-CHANK
NOW I'VE LOCKED YOU INSIDE.

BUT THAT WAS WRONG OF ME.
FOR A MOMENT, YOUR BIG SISTER SIMPLY WANTED TO PROTECT HER CUTE LITTLE SISTER WHO WAS BORN AT HER SIDE!
HOLD ON, I'LL LET YOU OUT.
HERE.
TUG
HUH?

TMP
IF YOU DIDN'T ALREADY KNOW...
...I'VE ALWAYS WANTED TO LOCK YOU UP LIKE THIS AND PROTECT YOU, PROTECT YOU, PROTECT YOU, AND BE KIND TO YOU.
I ALWAYS KNEW.
YET YOU'VE NEVER WANTED ME TO LOSE MY FREEDOM.
...
YOU KNEW.
OH
B-BUT THAT WAS JUST A FLEETING THOUGHT-THAT'S ALL. I'M NOT A WEIRDO OR ANYTHING.
BLUSH
DON'T BE SCARED!
I'M SURE YOU KNOW!!

DAMN...
HOW AWFUL... I WAS UN-ABLE TO RESTRAIN MYSELF FOR A SECOND.
SO THIS IS THE STRENGTH OF A PUREBLOOD VAMPIRE'S DESIRE!
I MUST SOOTHE THE MAD BEAST LAUGHING INSIDE ME!
YES...?
I'VE CALMED DOWN NOW!
REALLY ...?
OH MY. I ALMOST DESTROYED SOMETHING IMPORTANT IN A FIT OF PASSION...

I'VE DECIDED NOT TO LET YOU GO AFTER ALL.
THIS IS A CELL I PUT TOGETHER TO TRAP MOTHER AND ZERO INSIDE!!
AI...
BUT I NEVER PLANNED TO USE IT!
THEN...
AI...

OH.
KA-CHANK

WHEN WILL YOU HAVE THE DESIRE TO DRINK MY BLOOD, AI?
.....

LAST NIGHT, YOU...
...GAVE ME A LOT...
...THE ONE WHO ALWAYS RECEIVES FROM YOU.
I'M...
...
S...
SO...
WE...
WE WON'T BE ABLE TO SEE EACH OTHER FOR A WHILE, YOU KNOW?
AH.

MY LITTLE SISTER WOULD ALWAYS STAY BY MY SIDE AFTER I HAD DEALT WITH UNPLEASANT CASES LIKE THIS.
MY KIND AND PRECIOUS REN...
WELL THEN, AI...
...I PROMISE TO TRAIN HARD AND COME BACK STRONG.
I ASSUMED THAT YOU WOULD LOCK ME UP.
SHE WILL BE LEAVING ME FOR A WHILE.
SHE SAID THAT IN ORDER TO HELP ME, SHE WANTED TO BECOME MY "FINGERTIPS."

IT WAS MY MOTHER.

PLEASE STOP THOSE TRAITORS FROM USING THEIR BLOOD TO GIVE MORE POWER TO THE EMPIRE.

SPREAD THIS DECREE TO THE OTHER FORTS.
THE TRAITORS ARE TRYING TO FRAME US, BUT WE ARE UNITED. WE SHALL CRUSH THEIR AMBITION.
YES!
FOR BETTER OR FOR WORSE, THE FARCE FROM THAT DAY IS STILL IN EFFECT.

AFTER I SECRETLY MADE SURE THAT BOY HAD SAFELY JOINED...
...THE RESIS-TANCE ARMY...
A REPORT CAME IN THAT A TRAITOR HAD BEEN SEEN VISITING THE EMPIRE RECENTLY.
FOR A MOMENT I THOUGHT THE REPORT WAS ABOUT ME BECAUSE I HAD TAKEN THE BOY THERE, BUT IT WASN'T.

VAMPIRE
KNIGHT
MEMORIES
REN'S HONEY

I'VE COME TO ASK YOU IF THERE'S ANY POSSIBILITY OF PEACE BETWEEN US...
...IF I WERE TO BECOME THE FUTURE EMPEROR.
YET SHE WAS FAR MORE BEAUTIFUL THAN I REMEMBERED...

TEN YEARS HAVE PASSED SINCE THE RESISTANCE ARMY BECAME MY HOME.

I'VE NEVER FORGOTTEN THE WOMAN I MET BACK THEN. SHE'S REMAINED IN MY THOUGHTS.

IS IT POSSIBLE YOU'RE TARO...?
THE VAMPIRES ARE IN A LOCKDOWN, SO ANYONE WITH A ROOM THIS HUGE CAN'T BE AN ORDINARY VAMPIRE...
NOW THAT I THINK ABOUT IT.
WE WILL PROTECT YOU.
BUT IN RETURN, WE WILL NEED TO MAKE USE OF YOUR ROYAL STATUS WHEN THE TIME COMES.
TELL ME... WHY DID YOUR FATHER WANT YOU DEAD?

I WAS TOLD THAT THE QUEEN OF THE VAMPIRES HAS BEEN WAITING FOR ME HERE TOO.
SHE'S THE QUEEN, SO I SUSPECT SHE'S GOT REALLY THICK FANGS POKING OUT OF HER MOUTH.
AH...
I SEE.
...
YOU...?

AH...
LONG TIME NO SEE.
WHO ARE YOU?
WHAT?
UM...
I'M MEANT TO BE MEETING THE SUPPOSEDLY DEAD THIRD PRINCE OF THAT SCUMBAG EMPEROR.
I SUSPECT THE PRINCE WILL BE A STINKING AIRHEAD WITH A LEERING SMILE ON HIS FACE.

THAT WOMAN WAS STILL AS BEAUTIFUL AS WHEN I'D MET HER TEN YEARS AGO.

SHE'S WAITING INSIDE.

TEN YEARS PASSED.
...TO OVERTHROW THE EMPIRE WITH THE LEAST AMOUNT OF BLOODSHED POSSIBLE.
WITH THE AID OF A MYSTERIOUS COOPERATOR, THE RESISTANCE HAS BEEN GRADUALLY PREPARING...
AND—

Ai.

I SHOULD LOCK UP MY CUTE LITTLE SISTER SOMEWHERE...
AI...

THAT'S WHY I'M ASKING YOU, FATHER...
...TO PLEASE PROTECT AI WHILE I AM AWAY.

I WILL BECOME YOUR POWERFUL RIGHT-HAND WOMAN AND BE AT YOUR BECK AND CALL.

I AM A PATHETIC QUEEN.
AI, I'VE BEEN THINKING...
LET ME GO AND TRAIN SOMEWHERE FAR AWAY.

OUT THERE I WAS HIT AGAIN BY THE REALITY OF HOW AWFUL THE EMPIRE IS.
TO BE HONEST...
...I WANTED TO DO SOMETHING ABOUT IT MYSELF AT THAT VERY MOMENT...
THE POTENTIAL CONSEQUENCES OF THE CHOICES AT MY FINGERTIPS ARE FAR TOO SERIOUS FOR ME TO DECIDE AS I WISH.
...BUT IT WOULDN'T HAVE SOLVED THE OVERALL PROBLEM.

THOUGH IT HARDLY SEEMS TO MATTER.
TARO WILL SOON GROW UP AND THEN INTO AN OLD MAN...
...AND DISAPPEAR...
HMPH
IT MADE ME FEEL A LITTLE VEXED.
TARO MANAGED TO WIN YOUR TRUST IN ONLY A FEW DAYS.
AI...
YOU SEEM SAD.
WHAT'S TROUBLING YOU?

THANK YOU, REN.
I RECEIVED A REPORT. THE CONSTRUCTION MATERIAL WE SENT TO TOKIWA-SAMA WAS NEARLY STOLEN BY THE EMPIRE.
I MADE ARRANGEMENTS TO CHECK OUT THE DAMAGE WHILE YOU WERE AWAY.
I'M ONLY USEFUL AS A CARRIER PIGEON RIGHT NOW...
...SO YOU COULD'VE ALLOWED ME TO GO TO THE TOWN IN YOUR PLACE.
I'D NEVER ALLOW THAT.
IF YOU WERE SEEN AND ACCUSED OF SECRETLY WORKING FOR THE EMPIRE...
AI...
...I'D SERI-OUSLY LOSE MY TEMPER.
I DIDN'T ERASE TARO'S MEMORY.

AI.

I'M MARIA.
WELCOME TO THE RESISTANCE ARMY WE'RE CURRENTLY PREPARING...
...THIRD SON OF THE EMPEROR.

I'M NOT A SPY!
GET IN THERE!
THIS LADY WILL MEET YOU AND DECIDE WHETHER...
...YOU'RE A SPY.
YOU'RE WEL-COME HERE.
IT DOESN'T MATTER WHO YOU ARE...
...A SLAVE, A HUNTER, A VAM-PIRE...
...OR EVEN THE EMPEROR— AS LONG AS YOU'RE HERE TO FREE THE SLAVES.
KA-CHAK

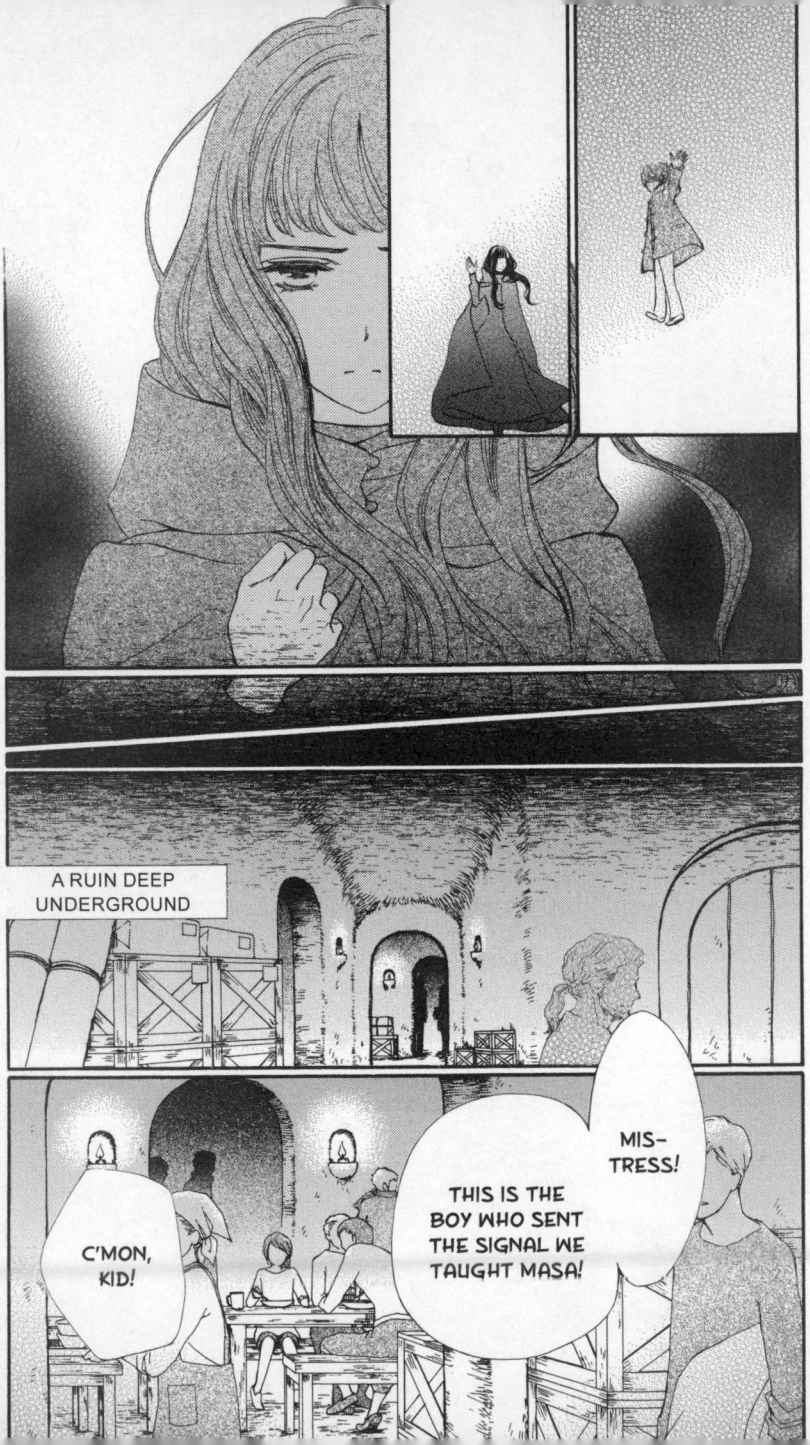
A RUIN DEEP UNDERGROUND
MIS-TRESS!
THIS IS THE BOY WHO SENT THE SIGNAL WE TAUGHT MASA!
C'MON, KID!

TAKE CARE OF YOUR-SELF...
...TARO.
MY NAME ISN'T TARO...
...BUT THAT'S OKAY.
YOU TAKE CARE TOO.

ABOUT THE MAN INSIDE THE COFFIN OF ICE.
I WON'T.
I DON'T KNOW WHY HE'S BEING PUNISHED...
...BUT...
...YOU CARE ABOUT HIM A LOT, RIGHT?
SUFF
SUFF
WHEW! I THOUGHT YOU WERE GOING TO SUCK MY BLOOD JUST THEN.
I WOULDN'T DO THAT.
HEH.

THANK YOU VERY MUCH FOR HELPING ME.
WAIT.
WHAT...?
LET ME TAKE A LOOK AT YOUR FACE ONE LAST TIME.
HEY...
PLEASE DON'T TELL ANYONE, WILL YOU?
I WANT TO REMEMBER IT.

I BET YOU THINK IT'S FUNNY.
EVERYONE BELIEVES THAT THESE MEASURES ARE NECESSARY TO PROTECT PUBLIC SAFETY...
...BECAUSE THE VAMPIRES ATTACKED US.
THE EMPEROR AND HIS FAMILY ARE THE BIGGEST SCUMBAGS OF ALL.
I USED TO BELIEVE THAT LIE TOO.
YOU BELIEVE WHAT I TOLD YOU?
...
YEAH...
BUT I STILL THINK VAMPIRES ARE MONSTERS.
I NEED TO GO NOW.
VAMPIRE LADY, YOU AREN'T MUCH LIKE A MONSTER.

AND THE SCUMBAGS AND THEIR FAMILIES WHO WISHED FOR THIS WORLD...
...ARE PROTECTED BY A WALL OF HUMANS LIVING IN THE CENTER OF THAT TOWN.

MASA...
IS THAT SOMEONE SPECIAL TO YOU?
YEAH.
...
MASA WAS JUST BEING KIND TO ME...
...BUT THEY ENSLAVED HER, AND NOW SHE'S GONE MISSING.

DAMN IT...
DAMN IT.
ALL I CAN DO IS WATCH OVER THEM...
...FOR NOW.
WELL...
I'LL BE FINE ON MY OWN.
I'VE SENT THE SIGNAL THAT MASA TAUGHT ME...
I NEED TO GO.

PEOPLE HAVE BEEN ENSLAVED.
THE OTHERS JUST WATCH SILENTLY BECAUSE THEY DON'T WANT TO BECOME SLAVES THEMSELVES.
AND THOSE WHO ARE IN CONTROL...
KLANK
KLANK
KLANK
KLANK
THEY'VE PASSED...
UH-HUH.
SWUP

THIS IS WHAT'S HAPPENING IN MY COUNTRY.
KLANK
KLANK

VAMPIRE
KNIGHT
MEMORIES
GRINDING TEETH

...THEN MONSTERS PROBABLY WANT TO BECOME ONE WITH HUMANS...
...I THINK.
I...
RIGHT.
...HUMANS AND MONSTERS CAN NEVER BE FRIENDS.
EVEN IF THAT'S TRUE...
...JUST WANTED TO VOICE THAT THOUGHT.
THE MONSTER LADY/END

WHEN THE MOON IS AT THE TOP OF THE SKY, I'M SUPPOSED TO GO TO THAT CERTAIN PLACE AND SEND A SIGNAL...
...TO MEET THE PEOPLE I WANT TO ASK FOR HELP.
THAT PLACE IS OUTSIDE THE CASTLE TOWN.
I MIGHT BE ABLE TO TAKE YOU THERE IF WE TAKE THE LONG WAY ROUND.
A THOUGHT STRUCK ME A LONG TIME AGO...
IF WE VAMPIRES ARE MONSTERS...
...AND VAMPIRES WANT TO BECOME ONE WITH THOSE THEY LOVE...

THANK YOU FOR HELPING ME.

AH.
THAT'S WHAT THIS LOOKS LIKE TO YOU.
I...
UM...
I KNOW YOU'RE NOT A MONSTER.
MONSTERS DON'T LOOK AT OTHER PEOPLE THE WAY YOU LOOK AT HIM...

DO IT
SOMETIMES WE MAKE THEM PAY WITH THEIR LIVES...
IS HE...
...BEING PUNISHED TOO?

ONCE YOUR MIND REGAINS THE STRENGTH IT ONCE HAD...
...YOUR LOVED ONE SHALL APPEAR IN YOUR MEMORIES ONCE AGAIN.
BUT THAT DOESN'T CHANGE THE FACT...
...THAT YOU ARE STILL A MONSTER!
YOU ATTACK PEOPLE!
THAT'S WHY YOU'RE BAD GUYS!
YOU PROBABLY WON'T BELIEVE ME...
...BUT WE'RE WORKING HARD NOT TO LET THOSE MONSTERS LOOSE IN THE WORLD.

VAMPIRES CAN ONLY QUENCH THEIR THIRST WITH THE BLOOD OF THEIR LOVED ONES...
...SO SOME WHO LOSE THE LOVE OF THEIR LIVES...
...END UP GOING INSANE.
IF YOU CAN STILL HEAR ME, YOU MUST LISTEN TO YOUR QUEEN.
FORGET EVERYTHING FOR NOW...

YOU'RE ALSO RIGHT THAT THERE ARE VAMPIRES WHO BECOME MONSTERS.
BUT...
THERE ARE THOSE WHO CHOOSE ...
...TO FALL INTO MADNESS...
...THOSE WHO SUCCUMB TO MADNESS AGAINST THEIR WILL...
...AND THOSE WHO HAVE LOST THEIR ONE AND ONLY PARTNER FOR LIFE...
...AFTER A SUDDEN ACCIDENT.

SOLT
YOU'RE PROBA-BLY TOO SCARED...
...TO BELIEVE WHAT I'M SAYING, BUT I'LL TELL YOU WHY.
WE DO IT TO BECOME ONE WITH THOSE WE LOVE.

YOU DON'T NEED TO BELIEVE ME IF YOU DON'T WANT TO.
...
...WHAT A BLOODSUCKING MONSTER SAYS?
HOW COULD I BELIEVE...
WHY DO YOU DRINK PEOPLE'S BLOOD?
I KNOW YOU PREPARE AND EAT ORDINARY MEALS TOO.

...AND KAIEN.
ALSO...
...TO TELL YOU THE TRUTH...
...MOST VAMPIRES AREN'T TOO HAPPY THAT THEIR ANCESTORS HAD WAGED...
...A STUPID WAR.

...
WHAT ...?
BUT...
...WE'RE NOT GOING TO FIGHT BACK SO EASILY.
WE'VE BEEN ENTRUSTED WITH THE HOPES AND EMOTIONS OF MANY PEOPLE...
...INCLUD-ING THOSE OF MY FATHER...
...YORI...

OKAY.
IF THAT'S TRUE, IT MUST'VE BEEN HARD FOR YOU TO TELL ME.
BUT YOU'RE MISTAKEN ABOUT ONE THING.
IT WAS THE HUMANS WHO ATTACKED US.

TARO...
ARE YOU A HUMAN CHILD WHO HAS BEEN ENSLAVED?
YES. THAT'S RIGHT.
I RAN AWAY...

...
A DOG HOLDING A KNIFE?
I'VE TOLD YOU! I GOT LOST AND WAS ATTACKED BY A WILD DOG.
...IS ALL YOUR FAULT.
...I GOT DRAGGED INTO THIS...
THE REASON...
...THEY WOULD'VE NEVER EVEN STARTED THAT ROTTEN EMPIRE.
IF YOU VAMPIRES HADN'T ATTACKED HUMANS IN THE FIRST PLACE...

PHOOO!
ALL DONE!
HEY...
W-WHAT ARE YOU DOING?! YOU DON'T NEED TO DO THAT!!
AHHH. I CAN'T TAKE THIS...
PLEASE LET ME GO...
NO.
WE DON'T KNOW ANYTHING ABOUT WHO ATTACKED YOU OR WHERE YOUR HOME IS...
...SO I CAN'T LET YOU GO AT THIS POINT.

AI, YOU'RE GOING TO QUESTION HIM...?
HEY!
I'LL TAKE CARE OF THAT!
NO, REN... HE'S MY RESPONSI-BILITY.
KREEE
YOU DON'T WANT AN IRRESPONSIBLE OLDER SISTER, DO YOU?
I WASN'T JUST ON THE DISCIPLINE COMMITTEE DURING MY HIGH SCHOOL DAYS. I ALSO WAS IN CHARGE OF CARING FOR THE ANIMALS!
AI...
RWL
RWL RWL
RWL

...I CAME ACROSS A STRAY ANIMAL AND BROUGHT HIM HOME.
NOW IT'S MY RESPONSIBILITY TO TAKE CARE OF YOU.
RWL
RWL
RWL
FIRST, THE POTTY!
HUH?
RWL
RWL
RWL
WHAT ?
THE TANK IS ABOVE AND BELOW...
KLATT
KLATT

I SEE.
BAD GUYS, HUH...
BUT...
THAT'S FINE. REGARDLESS...
...
...

I'D NEVER DO ANYTHING BAD.
I'M NOT LIKE YOU OR THEM—THE OTHER BAD GUYS.
...
SO WE'RE BAD GUYS TO YOU, TARO...?
THAT'S RIGHT!
ME AS WELL?
...
RIGHT ...
I KNOW YOU'RE ACTUALLY A BAD GUY.

ISN'T IT ABOUT TIME YOU TOLD ME YOUR NAME AND WHERE YOU LIVE?
I'M NOT SUPPOSED TO TALK TO ANYONE I DON'T TRUST.
THEN SHOULD I SECRETLY DROP YOU OFF IN FRONT OF THE EMPIRE POLICE STATION?
NO...
DID THEY BEAT YOU UP...
...BECAUSE YOU DID SOME-THING BAD?
I DIDN'T...

TARO...
YOU'VE BEEN HERE THREE DAYS NOW. WHAT DO YOU THINK?
DON'T CALL ME TARO.

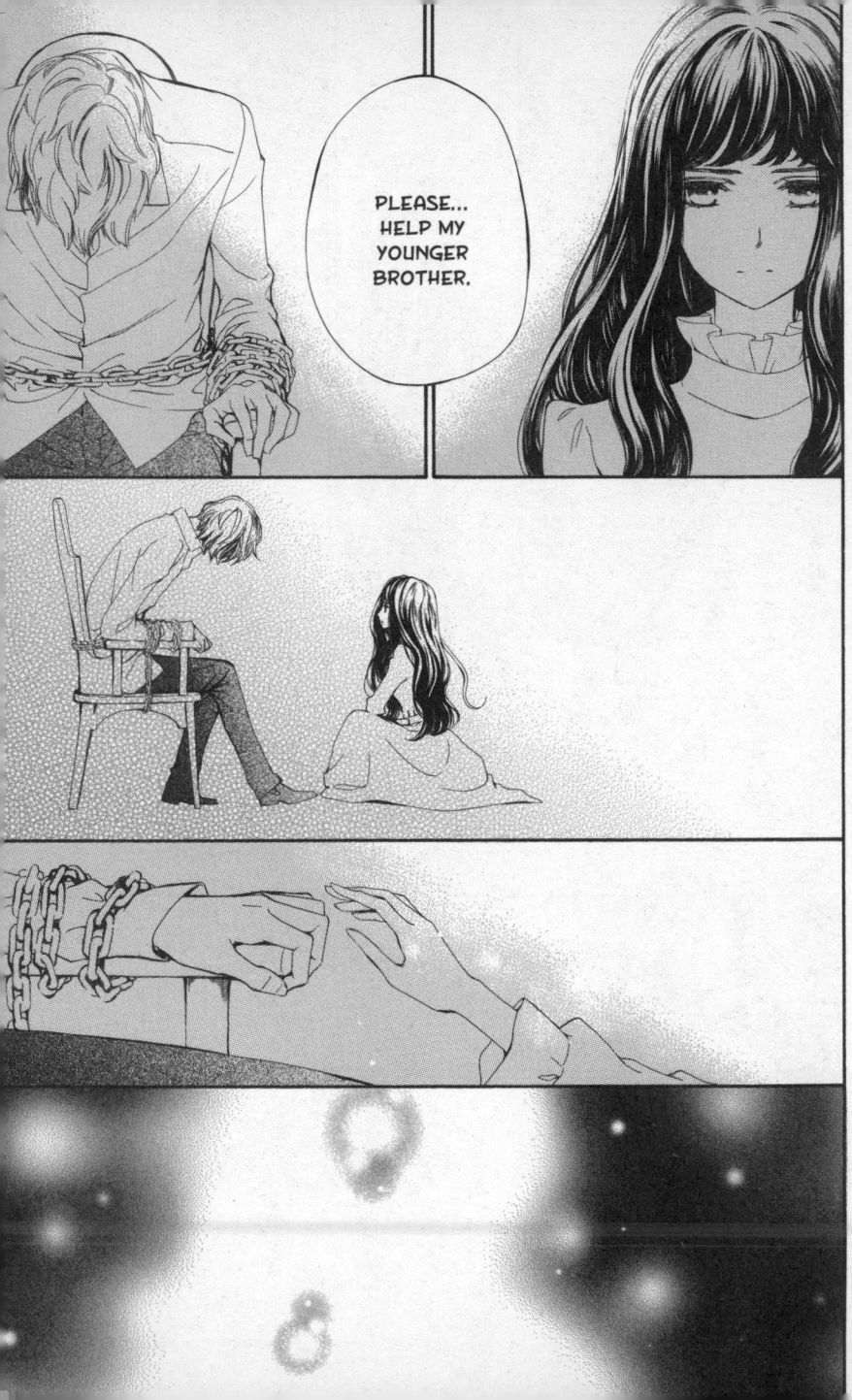
PLEASE... HELP MY YOUNGER BROTHER.

I HAD TO ATTEND TO MORE IMPORTANT DUTIES.
AH!
THANK YOU VERY MUCH.
I THOUGHT HE'D STILL BE ABLE TO HEAR YOU, AI-SAMA...
MY PLEA-SURE.
THIS WAY.
THIS IS THE MAIN REASON FOR ME BEING HERE.

HE WAS BADLY INJURED.
I WAS PLANNING TO LEAVE HIM SOMEWHERE SAFE ONCE I'D TREATED HIM.
YES...
THAT'S ALL THERE WAS TO IT.

A LONG TIME AGO, I FOUND A HUMAN BOY.

VAMPIRE
KNIGHT
MEMORIES
THE MONSTER LADY

...I CAN'T BE WITH YOU ALL THE TIME.
I WANT YOU TO STAY HERE BECAUSE IT'S THE SAFEST PLACE, AND IT COMES WITH FULL CHILDCARE.
NO, IT'S DANGEROUS HERE!
THEY'LL FREEZE ME TOO!!

TARO/END

COULD YOU TELL ME YOUR NAME AND WHERE YOU LIVE?
THAT'S OKAY.
I'LL JUST CALL YOU TAROU FOR NOW.
SORRY...
MAYBE VAMPIRES...
BUT...
...AREN'T...
...THAT DANGEROUS?

...
...?
HM?
SHE'S HELPING ME...?
WHAT...?

NO, DEAR.
I CAN'T LET YOU OUT ALONE.
SHE'S GOING TO EAT ME!!
I'LL LET YOU GO HOME.
BUT UNTIL THEN, YOU MUST STAY HERE WHERE IT'S SAFE.

NOOOOOO!!
HAVEN'T YOU EVER BEEN TAUGHT TO TREAT SOMEONE LIKE MY SISTER—WHO SAVED YOUR LIFE—WITH RESPECT, HUMAN?
!!
HE'S WOUNDED! HE'S WOUNDED AND HE'S JUST A CHILD!
THAT IS TRUE...
SHE'S GOING TO KILL ME!
YUP
I'VE GOT TO RUN AWAY!
VAMPIRES FEED ON...
...HUMANS!

TARO?
D-DON'T COME NEAR ME!
!!
YOU'RE A VAMPIRE, AREN'T YOU?!
TMP

SHE SMELLS LIKE EVENING DEW...
TARO... MAYBE "TAROU" WOULD'VE BEEN BETTER—
THAT'S NOT IMPORTANT.
AND IF ANYONE ASKS, I SHOULD SAY HE ISN'T TO BE TOUCHED BECAUSE HE'S THE SON OF AN OLD FRIEND OF YOURS, RIGHT?
AI...
I LOVE HOW YOU COULDN'T HELP BUT SAVE HIM.
OH MY. ♡
...
SHFF
AH. HE SEEMS TO HAVE WOKEN UP.

I'LL CALL YOU TARO FOR NOW.
NO...
THAT MAKES ME SOUND LIKE...
...A DOG.
EVENING DEW...

UP YOU GO!
WHAT'S YOUR NAME?
HUH?
I...
AH, RIGHT.
YOU PROBABLY DON'T FEEL LIKE TELLING ME FOR THE MOMENT BECAUSE YOU'RE INJURED.

SUUU
I'VE SUCKED AWAY YOUR PAIN.
HOLD ON A LITTLE LONGER.
LICK

...
AH.
YOU'RE BADLY INJURED.
IT MUST HURT...
IT'LL BE DIFFI-CULT...
...ONCE THE OTHERS NOTICE THE SCENT OF BLOOD.
...
OKAY...
YES.
SUFF
AH!
SORRY.

THUD
...
HUFF
!
ARE YOU ALL RIGHT ...?
...!!
A VAM...
SHUP
IT SEEMS NOT.
UHH...

YEAR 10149.
HUFF
HUFF
HUFF
THOK
Urk!
HUFF
HUFF

IT WON'T BE OF ANY USE TO US...
...IF WE ACT NOW.
NOT A SATIS-FYING ANSWER?
NO, IT ISN'T.
BUT...
...I KNOW YOU'RE MORE FRUSTRATED ABOUT THIS THAN ANYONE, AI.

THEY DON'T WANT OUR HELP.
TO THEM, VAMPIRES ARE THE ULTIMATE SYMBOL...
...OF INJUSTICE.
IF WE CHOOSE TO TAKE ACTION...
...OUR ADMINISTRATION WILL SURELY SPLIT IN TWO.

I DON'T KNOW HOW FAR WE CAN GET...
...WITHOUT INDISCRIMI-NATE ATTACKS.
CAN'T WE STOP THOSE HUMANS' ATROCITIES?
AI...?

IF YOU WANT TO LIVE...
...YOU MUST BECOME SLAVES TO THE CHOSEN ONES AND TO OUR GOOD CITIZENS.
YEAR 10140.
THE EMPIRE OF SAGES CAME INTO BEING.

I'M GOING TO GO SEE MY FRIEND WHO'S A MEMBER IN THE ASSEMBLY.
YOU STAY HOME WITH MOTHER.
POISON-ING THE RESER-VOIR...?
HOW COULD A WRETCHED METHOD LIKE THAT BE ALLOWED?
DADDY?
BAM
...HAS BEEN IMPRISON-ING CITIZENS...
...EVERY-WHERE.
I ACTED COURAGEOUSLY! I USED POISON TO FIGHT BACK AGAINST THE VAMPIRES!
HEY, I'M A HERO!

AI-SAMA.
WE'VE RECEIVED A REPORT FROM THOSE IN PURSUIT OF THE TRAITOR.
THE PUBLIC SECURITY FORCE—
THE PUBLIC SECURITY FORCE, WHO SHOULD BE PROTECTING HUMANS...

OKAY, THANK YOU.
NEXT, ABOUT FARMING...
YES.
I'VE BROUGHT YOU A PROPOSAL TONIGHT.
ARTI-FICIAL SUN-LIGHT?
YES.
WE'RE TAKING CONFERENCE NOTES...SO WHAT ARE YOU DOING?
UH-HUH. UH-HUH.
...
JUST JOTTING DOWN MY THOUGHTS AND IDEAS.
I'M STUDY-ING.
SKRTCH SKRTCH
NEXT IS—

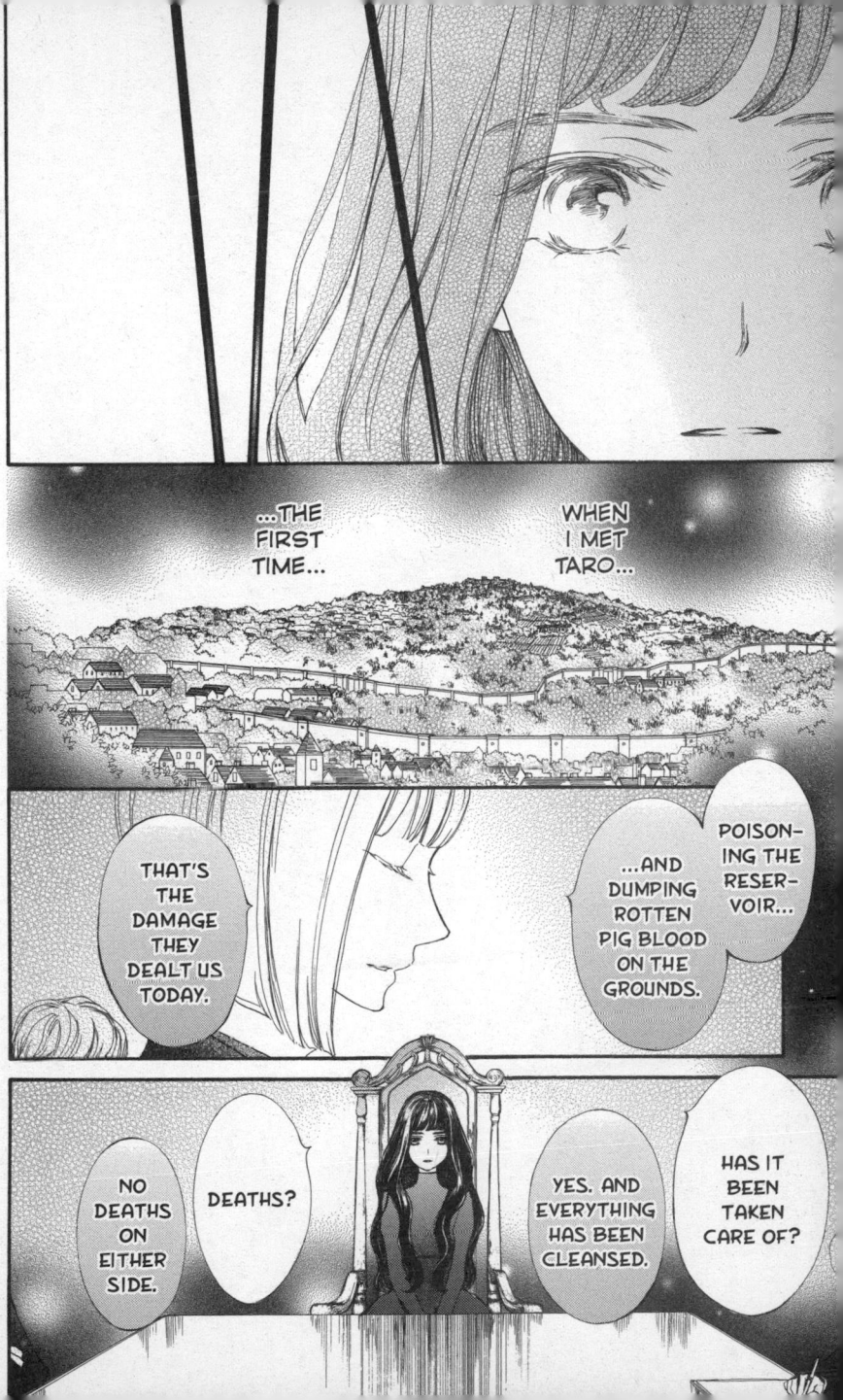
...THE FIRST TIME...
WHEN I MET TARO...
THAT'S THE DAMAGE THEY DEALT US TODAY.
...AND DUMPING ROTTEN PIG BLOOD ON THE GROUNDS.
POISONING THE RESERVOIR...
NO DEATHS ON EITHER SIDE.
DEATHS?
YES. AND EVERYTHING HAS BEEN CLEANSED.
HAS IT BEEN TAKEN CARE OF?

TARO...?

I NEED YOUR HELP!
IT HAS TO BE YOU!

AFTER YOU.
CHAK
...!

PERSONALLY I DON'T AGREE WITH IT, BUT MY HANDS ARE TIED.
...
AH...
I SMELL BLOOD FROM SOMEONE MOVING...
IS SOMEONE IN THE BACK?
I CALLED YOU HERE BECAUSE I WANTED YOU TO MEET HIM.
HE MUST'VE WOKEN UP.

FOR NOW, WE NEED SOMEONE TO KEEP AN EYE ON HIM AT ALL TIMES.
IT'S FINE.
HE'S STILL IN A RATHER UNSTABLE STATE.
OTHERWISE SOMEONE LIKE ME MAY TRY TO DO SOMETHING TO HIM JUST FOR FUN.
I KNOW YOU'VE BEEN ASKED...
...TO GIVE HIM SOME TIME...

SORRY.
I KNOW IT'S AN IMPORTANT TIME FOR YOU.
THAT'S OKAY. I'M ASKING YOU TO DO A LOT OF THINGS FOR US.
YOU CALLED FOR ME, SO HERE I AM.
SORRY FOR CAUSING YOU SO MUCH TROUBLE.
I HAVE A RATHER DIFFICULT AGENDA RIGHT NOW AS A SUBSTITUTE LIAISON.
I'M GLAD YOU SAY THAT.

WE WERE ABLE TO ESTABLISH THIS SMALL NATION...
...THANKS TO YOUR SUPPORT.
MAY I...
...ASK YOU FOR A FAVOR?

THANK YOU...
...VERY MUCH...
...FOR YOUR LONG YEARS AS THE GRAVE KEEPER.

VAMPIRE
KNIGHT
MEMORIES
TARO

THE PATH THAT LEADS TO YOU/END

I'LL GO ON.
YOU RETURN THE WAY WE CAME.
NO.
A CHIM-NEY...
THAT MIGHT HAVE BEEN AIMED AT YOU.
I CAN AT LEAST SHIELD YOU...

YOU WAIT BACK AT HOME!
AI IS PROBABLY— NO, SHE'LL DEFINITELY BE FINE!
I'M GOING DOWN TO GET HER.
IT'S BEEN SOME TIME AND SHE STILL HASN'T COME BACK...
NO.
KRUK
REN!
BUT...
OH

YES.
YOU'RE FASTER THAN I AM.
YOU GO ON AHEAD.

YOU'RE RIGHT...
WE'RE ACCOM-PLICES.
IT'S OUR DUTY TO PAY OUR DEBT TOGETHER.
WE HAVE TO DO SOMETHING ABOUT THIS FOR AI AND REN'S SAKE.

WHAT ARE...
...WE?

...
THIS IS MY FAULT.
NO.
EVEN IF IT TAKES MY LIFE, I'LL HUNT THEM DOWN MYSELF.
IT'S NOTH-ING...
HEY!

...BUT I HOPE THIS LIFE TORMENTS YOU FOR ETERNITY.
ZERO?
HUH...?
WHAT IS IT?
DID YOU REMEMBER SOMETHING?

WHAT?
WAIT.
WE SHARE A COMMON GOAL, DON'T WE?
YOU'RE NOT GOING START WITH ME?!
YOU KILL PURE-BLOODS!
I JUST CAME TO CHECK YOUR CELL BEFORE I LEAVE ON A JOURNEY.
...WHETHER HE MADE A MISTAKE OR WAS SIMPLY LAZY...
I DON'T KNOW THE REASON KANAME KURAN KEPT YOU ALIVE...

WHAT DO THE MAYOR AND OTHERS WANT?
DO I EVEN NEED TO TELL YOU?
THE POWERS HELD WITHIN A VAMPIRE'S BLOOD ATTRACTED THEIR GREED AND CAUSED THIS STRIFE.
NOTHING NEW, IS IT?
TELL ME THE TRUTH.
YOU AGREE, DON'T YOU?
VAMPIRES NEED TO BE ANNIHILATED.

...ZERO KIRYU.
YOU'RE AN ODDITY AS A VAMPIRE AND HUNTER. IT WAS YOUR FLESH AND BLOOD...
...THAT GAVE BIRTH TO THOSE HYBRIDS.
THOSE MASTERMINDS WERE SO GRATEFUL THAT YOU GOT CAUGHT WITHOUT A FIGHT!

ME?
I PROMISED TO SAVE THE DAUGHTER OF ONE OF THE MASTERMINDS IN RETURN FOR A LEISURELY LIFE HERE.
I PROVIDED SOME OF MY FLESH AND BLOOD FOR SOME WEIRDO SCIENTIST'S RESEARCH, BUT THE SAMPLE TURNED OUT TO BE USELESS.
OH, RIGHT. I CONTROLLED THE TREE ROOTS TO HELP THAT MAN TOO...
TWRL
AH.
I CAN'T DO ANYTHING BECAUSE OF...
...KANAME KURAN'S CURSE...
MMBL MMBL
NOTHING AT ALL.
I JUST TOOK PART IN A LITTLE SCHEME, AND I END UP IN THIS HELLHOLE.
MMBL MMBL
MMBL MMBL
AND YOU...!
GLARE
I'M SO JEALOUS YOU GET TO DO WHAT YOU WANT...

I FINALLY...
...GET TO TALK WITH YOU ALONE.
LET ME GET STRAIGHT TO THE POINT.
YOU LET YOUR GUARD DOWN.
IT'S ALL YOUR FAULT...
...MORE OR LESS.

DO YOU REMEMBER...?
HEY, YUKI.
IT WAS THAT KIDNAPPING CASE THAT MOTIVATED US TO GET MARRIED.
YES? WHAT IS IT?
I MESSED UP...
...DURING THAT INCIDENT.
UH-HUH.
...AND I WAS UNABLE TO NOTICE WHO WAS CONTROLLING THE "ROOTS"— THE ONE RESPONSIBLE FOR TAKING THAT SCIENTIST AWAY.
MY HEAD WAS FILLED WITH RAGE...
...I REALIZED IT WAS THE MAN WHO HAD TURNED ME INTO A TATTERED RAG.
SOMETIME AFTER THE CULPRIT WAS CAPTURED...

HELLOOOO? CAN YOU HEAR ME?
AND...
POIT
...IF HE WERE PLANNING TO COMPLAIN, HE SHOULD'VE DONE SO BEFORE HE LEFT US.

RIGHT...
I SHOULD PUT IT AWAY.
THAT GUN IS A PRECIOUS ITEM.

OKAY, ZERO KIRYU, IT'S ABOUT TIME WE HAD A LONG CHAT!
THEY'RE MORE MATURE THAN YOU, SO I COULDN'T HELP IT...
HEY, THAT'S WHAT YOU DO TO OUR DAUGHTERS!

POFF
SHFF
SHFF

...
BUT IF...
NO.
I WISH WE COULD'VE TAKEN THE TIME TO SHOW THE HEAD-MASTER OUR WEDDING...
YEAH.
EVEN IF HE HAD GIVEN US A SIGN MEANING "NO"...
...WE'D HAVE STILL GONE THROUGH WITH IT.

THAT QUIET MOMENT...
...ENDED UP BECOMING OUR SECRET WEDDING.

WE WAITED FOR HIM...
...TO GIVE US HIS PERMISSION TO MARRY.

THE TWO OF US WERE WAITING FOR A SIGN...
...ON THAT DAY TOO, WEREN'T WE?
I GUESS SO.

...
WHY AREN'T YOU SLEEPING? WHAT ARE YOU DOING?
I'VE ALWAYS WON-DERED...
POKE
POKE
POKE
POKE
WE KNOW THAT PART OF HIM MERGED WITH YOUR BLOODY ROSE...
...SO MAYBE IF WE STIMULATED IT IN SOME WAY...
YOU THINK HE'D APPEAR BEFORE YOU AS A PHANTOM AGAIN...?
HMM.
I WONDER.

...WE'VE BEEN ACCOM-PLICES...
...EVER SINCE THAT SECOND NIGHT...
...IN YOUR ROOM AT THE DORM, ZERO...

YOU'RE THE REPRESENTATIVE OF THE HUNTER SOCIETY! ARE YOU IN ANY POSITION TO BE DOING SOMETHING LIKE THIS?!
WHY AM I GETTING SCOLDED?
WHAT?
HMPH!
WHY DID YOU HAVE TO MEET UP WITH ME SO EARLY?!
TUG
WE'VE ALWAYS BEEN REGARDED AS ACCOMPLICES.
C'MON.
IT'S TOO LATE FOR SECOND THOUGHTS.
IT'S TRUE...
YES...
YOU'RE RIGHT.
WE NEED TO FIND SOMEPLACE TO HIDE BEFORE SUNRISE.

THAT'S THE TOWN THAT WAS BURIED UNDER SAND TEN THOUSAND YEARS AGO.
DISASTER FELL FROM THE SKY...
...
...AND CREATED THIS CIRCULAR DESERT BELT.
WHY'D YOU CUT A LONG STORY SHORT?
I ALWAYS SLEPT DURING GEOGRAPHY CLASS, SO I CAN'T TRULY EXPLAIN HOW IT HAPPENED!
SORRY!

...SEARCHING FOR HER TRAIL.
YOU TWO WON'T TELL ME EVERY-THING...
...SO I'LL CON-TINUE...
THE EVENTS YOU HAVEN'T TOLD ME ABOUT...
THAT WOMAN AND THE OTHERS I LEFT BEHIND...

TODAY...
...
WHAT IS IT?
NOTHING.
I CAN'T ALLOW ANYTHING TO HAPPEN TO YOU WHEN AI ISN'T AROUND.
I'M THINKING ABOUT WANDERING AROUND TOWN TODAY.
YOU'RE GOING TO KEEP AT IT, RIGHT?
I SEE. THEN I'LL JOIN YOU.
TMP

AREN'T YOU...
...OPENING THE SHOP TODAY?

YOU KNOW...
...I DID EVERYTHING I COULD.
I WONDER IF THIS PATH...
...LEADS TO YOU...

SEND THE ELITE FORCES AFTER HER!
CAPTURE HER AND BRING HER TO JUSTICE!

THE VAMPIRES HAVE LOCKED THEMSELVES UP IN THEIR TERRITORY.
THE SO-CALLED PUBLIC SECURITY FORCE WILL BE DOING THE JOB OF VAMPIRE HUNTERS.
SO...
...WE'LL BE SHUTTING DOWN THAT PART OF THE HUNTER SOCIETY'S...
...FUNC-TIONS.

SHE BETRAYED US!

VAMPIRE
KNIGHT
MEMORIES
THE PATH THAT LEADS TO YOU

VAMPIRE KNIGHT MEMORIES

CONTENTS

The Path That Leads to You 5

Taro 37

The Monster Lady 69

Grinding Teeth 97

Ren's Honey 127

The Path That Leads to You: Dash! 158

Editor's Notes 159

KANAME KURAN

A pureblood vampire and the progenitor of the Kurans. He is Yuki's fiancé and was raised as her sibling. He threw his heart into the furnace to become the ancestor metal for weapons that would kill vampires.

ZERO KIRYU

He was born into a family of vampire hunters and later was turned into a vampire. He had a strong hatred toward vampires, but he decided to live his life with Yuki.

REN AND AI

Yuki's children

HANABUSA AIDO

He was an upperclassman in the Night Class. He is working to create a medicine that will turn vampires into humans...

The Story of VAMPIRE KNIGHT

Previously...

At the End of *Vampire Knight*

- Kaname had been planning to kill all purebloods in order to protect Yuki, but he chose to entrust the future to Yuki and Zero instead. He threw his heart into the furnace, and that became the ancestor metal used to create weapons capable of killing vampires. He then slept in a coffin of ice.
- A thousand years later, Yuki gave her life to revive Kaname as a human being. Ren and Ai deliver the words Yuki left to Kaname...

***Vampire Knight: Memories* Begins**

- Kaname has lost his memory after being revived after a thousand years. Kaname desires to know what happened with the woman he can't quite remember, so his daughters begin to tell him stories from the past thousand years.
- During the time Kaname was in the coffin of ice, the split between humans and vampires widened. In order to prevent the worst possible outcome—a massacre of the humans by the vampires—Yuki took on the role of a "traitor" and disappeared. Zero followed her, and the two began their journey. Ai, who was entrusted with the rest, lead the vampires to isolate themselves from the outside world...

CHARACTERS

YUKI KURAN (CROSS)

The adopted daughter of the headmaster of Cross Academy. She is a pureblood vampire and the princess of the noble Kuran family. She has always adored Kaname, even when she did not have her memory.

VAMPIRE KNIGHT
MEMORIES

VOLUME
7

STORY & ART BY
Matsuri Hino